CHI

4/99

Learning About Your Health

Bruises

By

David H. Hundley

ROURKE PRESS, INC.
VERO BEACH, FLORIDA 32964

Printed in the United States of America.

Library of Congress Cataloging-in-Publication Data

Hundley, David H., 1946-
    Bruises / David H. Hundley
       p.   cm. — (Learning about your health)
Summary: Discusses the nature, causes, and treatment of bruises, as well as how to avoid them.
    ISBN 1-57103-254-1
    1. Bruises—Juvenile literature. 2. Children—Wounds and injuries—Juvenile literature. 3. First aid in illness and injury—Juvenile literature. [1. Bruises. 2. Wounds and injuries. 3. First aid.]   I. Title.
II. Series.
RD93.5.C4H86   1998
617.1'3—dc21   98-7655
                                                     CIP
                                                       AC

Photographs: Cover, pp. 7, 17, 21 © PhotoDisc; pp. 5, 13, 25, 27, © RubberBall Productions; pp. 9, 12, 18, 19, 20, 23, © Adobe Systems Incorporated.

Contents

Crash!

You are playing soccer. You are running down the field toward the goal. A player on the other team is running next to you. The ball is coming your way. You run toward it. The player next to you runs toward it. You collide and both crash to the field. When you get home and undress you notice a blue-black spot on your hip. You have a **bruise** (brews).

Bruises are common
when playing sports
like soccer.

What Is a Bruise?

A bruise is blood in the tissue (tish-shoe) under the skin. It appears at a spot where you fell, bumped, or were hit. It can be painful or not hurt at all. It is caused by many small broken blood vessels. It is also called a contusion (kun-too-shun).

You have probably had bruises on your shins and arms. Bruises are usually a black-purple color. As time passes, they fade. They may turn a yellow-brown color as the blood disolves and then disappear.

Placing an ice pack on a bruise helps to reduce swelling.

How Do I Get a Bruise?

Most children are used to having bruises. They are usually the result of an accident (**ak**-sid-ent). You can fall from your bicycle. You can bump into a desk at school. You can run into another child playing sports. Bruises can appear anywhere on your body. Bruises usually happen where there is a bone under the skin. They happen less in soft parts of the body.

You can get a
bruise from falling
off a tricycle or
bicycle.

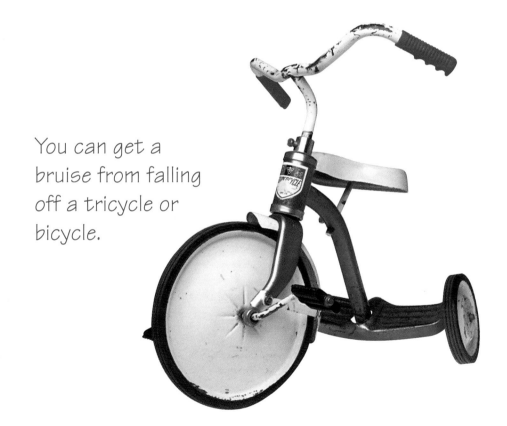

The Cardiovascular System

The **cardiovascular** (car-dee-oh-**vask**-cue-lure) **system** is the heart, **arteries** (**are**-tur-ease), **veins** (**vanes**), and lungs. The heart pumps blood to the arteries. The arteries move blood through our body. Veins bring blood back to the heart. The lungs add oxygen to the blood before it returns to the arteries. It is also called the **circulatory** (**cirk**-cue-lah-tory) **system** because it circulates blood through the body.

Blood circulates, or moves, deep inside the body and near the surface of the skin. It delivers nutrients (**new**-tree-ants) and oxygen (**ox**-e-gin) to parts of the body and returns the blood to be loaded with nutrients and oxygen again before the next circulation. You might think of the circulatory system as a system of tubes, a filter, and a pump.

Veins and Arteries

Some veins and arteries are large. Others are very small. Imagine what happens to the small ones when they are hit hard with only the thin layer of skin to protect them. If you are playing baseball and are hit by the ball, you will bruise.

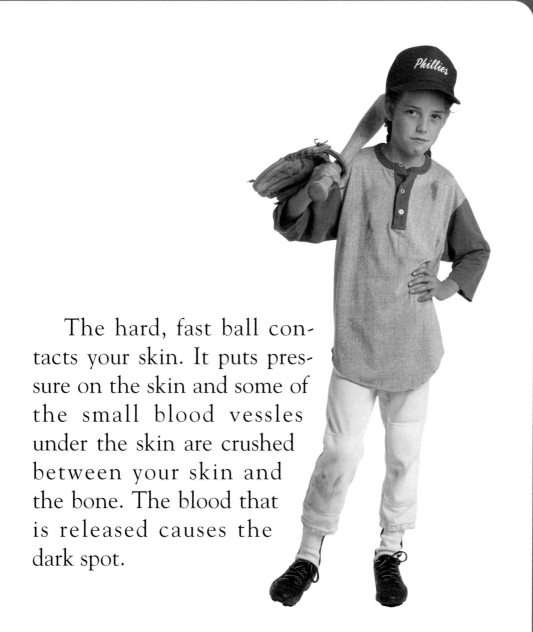

The hard, fast ball contacts your skin. It puts pressure on the skin and some of the small blood vessles under the skin are crushed between your skin and the bone. The blood that is released causes the dark spot.

What Is Swelling?

Most bruises are caused by accidents or sports injuries. Bruises you get from a sports injury might be accompanied by swelling. Swelling means blood is flowing into an injured part of your body. The blood helps to heal the injury.

Remember RICE for treating a sports injury.

R   **REST. Stop playing.**

I   **ICE. Apply ice to the injury to stop swelling.**

C   **COMPRESSION. Apply light pressure to stop bleeding. Wrap with an elastic bandage.**

E   **ELEVATE. Raise the injured part above the heart to stop bleeding and swelling.**

What Is a "Black Eye?"

A "black eye" is a bruise of the cheek, eyelid, and eyebrow. It is a common sports injury. It also is a common accident injury. If you fall or are thrown against the ground or a wall, your face will probably be the first thing to hit.

If you have a black eye, you should put an ice pack on it right away to reduce the swelling. Then you should visit a doctor to see if your eye is okay. The doctor will find

A black eye is a common
sports injury.

out if there
is anything
in your eye,
if the eyeball
is injured, or if
you simply bruised
the cheek, eyebrow, and
eyelid. The black eye will heal in a couple
of weeks.

Cuts and Scrapes

When you bruise yourself, you also might cut or scrape your skin. A cut is a slice of the skin's surface. You will usually bleed from a cut. You must get help if you have a deep cut.

Putting a band-aid over a small cut or scrape helps avoid infection.

A scrape is something you have probably had many times. It is when you fall or rub against a rough surface, such as cement. It will leave the skin rough with just a little blood in spots. You should clean the skin as soon as possible to avoid infection (in-**feckt**-shun).

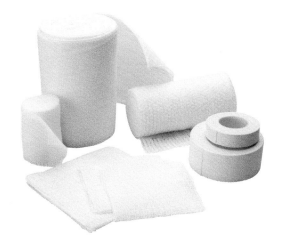

Tape and gauze can be used to protect a wound.

Punctures

A puncture (**punkt-sure**) is a hole in the skin made by an object such as a scissors or fence post. Do not remove the object from the wound until the doctor arrives. If you have a puncture wound, make yourself comfortable.

A sharp object such as a pair of scissors can puncture the skin.

Ask someone to telephone 911 so help will come. A puncture can cause deep bleeding. You may not see it. A doctor can examine you and see if there is bleeding inside your body.

A puncture can be serious. You may need to call for emergency help.

Bleeding

Sometimes the accidental bump that causes a bruise might also cut the skin. In that case blood will be trapped in tissue beneath the skin. It also will flow out of the wound. If you have a minor cut, you can put pressure on the wound to stop the bleeding. Take a clean cloth and lightly press on the wound.

The body sends blood to the wound to form a scab. The scab closes the wound. The bleeding stops. Once the bleeding stops, clean the wound and apply a loose bandage to keep it clean.

It is a good idea to
have a first aid kit
on hand in case of
an accident.

Head Injuries

The body delivers a lot of blood to the scalp (**skalp**). If you get hit in the head you probably will develop a bruise. You might also develop an "egg," or hematoma (hem-ma-**toe**-ma). A bump will form where you were hit. This bump is filled with blood. You should apply an ice pack to reduce the swelling.

Your parents will watch you for signs of sudden sleepiness, numbness, or change in your eyes if you get hit in the head. They will ask you to rest but not go to sleep for a few hours. If no symptoms (**sim-tums**) appear, they will let you sleep. They will relax after you get a good night's sleep.

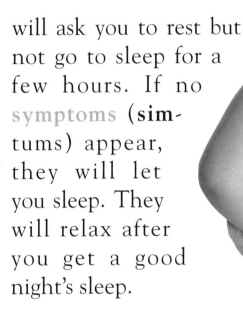

It is important to not go to sleep right away if you get hit in the head.

You Can Prevent Bruises, Cuts, and Scrapes

You can prevent some bruises by being careful. Sit down carefully. Do not throw yourself into a chair. Open doors carefully. Walk straight through openings. Watch where you are running. Do not collide with others.

When playing sports, wear **protective** (pro-**tekt**-eve) gear. You can wear a helmet when you ride a bicycle to avoid head

injury. You can wear elbow pads, knee pads, and gloves when you roller skate or roller blade. If you fall down you will not cut, scrape or bruise yourself as often.

Glossary

accident (**ak**-sid-ent) - something you do not expect to happen. A fall from a tree is an accident.

arteries (**are**-tur-ease) - the tubes in your body that move blood from the heart through your body.

bruise (**brews**) - a dark spot undet the skin; an injury makes blood collect under the skin.

cardiovascular (car-dee-oh-**vask**-cue-lure) **system** - the body system made of the heart, veins, and lungs. It moves blood and oxygen through the body.

contusion (kun-**too**-shun) - a bruise; broken blood vessels under the skin.

hematoma (hem-ma-**toe**-ma) - an egg-shaped bump filled with blood that forms when you hit your head.

lungs - the parts of the body in your chest that take oxygen from the air you breathe and add it to your blood.

nutrients (**new**-tree-ants) - things that are necessary for growth and life. Fruits and vegetables have many nutrients.

oxygen (**ox**-e-gin) - a natural element that the body takes from the air and delivers to the cells.

protective (pro-**tekt**-eve) - something that prevents injury. A football helmet is protective gear.

puncture (**punkt**-sure) - a hole in the skin made by a blunt object. If you poke your hand with a pencil it can make a puncture wound.

scalp - the skin on your head.

swell - to become large after an injury. When you sprain an ankle it swells.

symptoms (**sim**-tums) - changes in your body or behavior that are signs of an injury or illness.

tissue (**tish**-shoe) - the soft body material under the skin.

veins (**vanes**) - the tubes in your body that move blood from your body back to the heart.

For More Information

Children's Healthwatch from Mayo Clinic. http://healthfront.com

Grolier Encyclopedia of Science and Technology. Danbury, CT: Grolier Educational Corporation, 1994.

Health Infopark. http://www.merck.com

Kingfisher Children's Encyclopedia. New York: Kingfisher Books, 1992.

Raintree Steck-Vaughn Illustrated Science Encyclopedia. Austin, TX: Steck-Vaughn, 1997.

Rourke's World of Science Encyclopedia. Vero Beach, FL: Rourke Corporation, Inc., 1998.

The World Book Encyclopedia. Chicago: World Book, Inc., 1998.

Index